JANE AUSTEN'S
KITCHEN

A Feast Through Austen's World

Step into a world where elegance, wit, and culinary delights converge. In the pages that follow, we invite you to embark on a gastronomic journey through the enchanting era of Jane Austen. As we turn the pages of her timeless novels, we also unveil the secrets of the Regency kitchen, where each dish tells a tale of opulence, tradition, and the artistry of a bygone culinary era.

The Regency era, with its dance cards and societal intricacies, is not just a chapter in history; it's a feast waiting to be savored. In this cookbook, we traverse the delicate dance of flavors that once graced the tables of Austen's characters. From the bustling kitchens of grand estates to the modest hearths of country homes, our culinary adventure aims to capture the essence of Regency dining—a delightful symphony of taste, tradition, and refined sensibilities. As you flip through these pages, envision yourself in a sunlit drawing room, surrounded by the genteel company of characters who have captured the hearts of readers for centuries. Each recipe is a culinary portrait, inspired by the personalities and settings of Austen's novels. From the practicality of Elinor Dashwood to the romantic spirit of Marianne, every dish embodies the essence of its literary muse.

But this book is more than a collection of recipes. It is an ode to a time when the clinking of silverware and the flicker of candlelight set the stage for social gatherings. From the gleam of polished silverware to the delicate touch of lace on the tablecloth, we pay homage to the aesthetics and etiquette that defined Regency dining.

Throughout these pages, you will find not just instructions but an invitation—to revive the rituals of afternoon tea, to savor the simplicity of hearty stews, and to partake in the elegance of grand banquets. We explore the unique cooking methods, the seasonal abundance of ingredients, and the meticulous table settings that made every meal a celebration.

So, unfold your napkin, embrace the echoes of Austen's world, and immerse yourself in a culinary tapestry woven with history, literature, and the unmistakable flavors of the Regency era. May each recipe transport you to a time when meals were a poetic expression, and every bite carried the weight of tradition.

In the spirit of Jane Austen's enduring legacy, let this cookbook be your guide to hosting a feast fit for characters in corsets and cravats—where the clatter of cutlery echoes the laughter of Elizabeth Bennet, and the aroma of delicacies fills the air with the warmth of Elinor Dashwood's hearth.

THE REGENCY ERA: A CULINARY TAPESTRY

The early 19th century, known as the Regency era, was a period of transition marked by cultural, social, and political shifts. As we embark on this culinary journey through Jane Austen's world, understanding the historical context enriches our appreciation for the flavors and traditions that shaped the dining tables of the time.

1. Social Hierarchy: Regency society was stratified, with clear divisions between the upper, middle, and lower classes. This hierarchy extended to dining, influencing not only the types of food consumed but also the manner in which it was served. Elaborate banquets in grand estates contrasted with simpler, more practical meals in middle-class households.

2. The Role of Household Staff: In wealthy households, an extensive staff managed the day-to-day operations of the estate, including the kitchen. Cooks, kitchen maids, and scullery maids worked in unison to produce the diverse and often lavish meals expected by the upper class. The dynamics of the kitchen reflected the intricate social structures of the time.

3. Open Hearth Cooking: The heart of the Regency kitchen was the open hearth, where most cooking took place. Large cauldrons, spits, and griddles were positioned over the flames, offering a versatile cooking environment. Spit roasting was a common method for cooking large cuts of meat, showcasing the ingenuity of the era's culinary techniques.

4. Seasonal and Local Ingredients: Access to ingredients was influenced by the seasons and geographic location. Menus were shaped by what was available locally, and preserving methods like salting and pickling were employed to extend the shelf life of certain foods. The use of fresh, seasonal produce was a hallmark of Regency cuisine.

5. Culinary Innovations: The Regency era witnessed culinary innovations, with the introduction of new cooking techniques and equipment. Mechanical roasting jacks, powered by clockwork mechanisms, automated the turning of spits in wealthier households. Copper cookware gained popularity for its excellent heat conductivity.

6. Formal Dining Etiquette: Formal dining was a highly ritualized affair, governed by strict etiquette. Courses were served sequentially, and table manners were a reflection of social standing. The placement of dishes on the table and the manner in which they were presented became an art form, emphasizing the importance of aesthetics in dining.

7. Tea Culture: Tea played a central role in Regency social life. Afternoon tea, introduced by Anna, the Duchess of Bedford, became a fashionable social event. Delicate finger sandwiches, scones, and pastries accompanied by a variety of teas were served in elegant settings, shaping the iconic British tea culture.

8. Evolution of Culinary Literature: The Regency era witnessed the rise of culinary literature. Cookbooks became increasingly popular, providing not only recipes but also insights into proper household management. The emergence of gastronomic literature reflected a growing interest in the art and science of cooking.

As we explore the recipes inspired by Jane Austen's novels, these historical insights serve as guideposts, offering glimpses into the culinary landscape of the Regency era. Let the flavors of the past come alive as we step back in time and savor the tastes that defined this remarkable period.

Austen's Culinary Canvas
Regency-Inspired Recipes

9. Persuasion Picnic: Seaside Delicacies with Anne Elliot
   - Captain Wentworth's Seafood Pâté
   - Lyme Regis Lobster Salad
   - Admiral Croft's Ginger Beer
10. Bath Assembly Bakes: Delicacies from Northanger Abbey
   - Catherine Morland's Lavender Shortbread
   - Tilney's Tea Cakes
   - Eleanor's Elderflower & Lemon Madeleines
11. Dashwood Desserts: Sweet Temptations from Sense and Sensibility
   - Marianne's Honeyed Almonds
   - Colonel Brandon's Dark Chocolate Mousse
   - Elinor's Orange Blossom Cake
12. Emma's Garden Feast: Seasonal Delights from Highbury
   - Mr. Woodhouse's Cucumber Mint Sandwiches
   - Mr. Knightley's Asparagus and Lemon Risotto
   - Hartfield Herb-infused Lemonade
13. Regency Revelry Cocktails: Libations for Social Soirées
   - Ballroom Punch with Rose Petal Ice Cubes
   - Pimm's Cup for a Summer Garden Party
   - Mr. Bingley's Blackberry Bramble
14. Beyond the Ballroom: Late-Night Nibbles for Austen-Inspired Gatherings
   - Midnight Macarons with Lavender Ganache
   - Sir Walter Elliot's Truffle Oil Popcorn
   - Wickham's Whiskey-infused Nuts

Morning Repast at Longbourn: Breakfasts with the Bennets

MRS. BENNET'S BERRY SCONES

Ingredients:

- 2 cups all-purpose flour
- 1/3 cup granulated sugar
- 1 tablespoon baking powder
- 1/2 teaspoon salt
- 1/2 cup unsalted butter, cold and cut into small cubes
- 1 cup mixed berries (such as blueberries, raspberries, and strawberries), fresh or frozen
- 2/3 cup heavy cream
- 1 teaspoon vanilla extract
- Zest of one lemon

Instructions:

1. Preheat your oven to 400°F (200°C) and line a baking sheet with parchment paper.
2. In a large bowl, whisk together the flour, sugar, baking powder, and salt.
3. Add the cold butter to the dry ingredients and use your fingers or a pastry cutter to incorporate it until the mixture resembles coarse crumbs.
4. Gently fold in the mixed berries, lemon zest, heavy cream, and vanilla extract until just combined.
5. Turn the dough out onto a lightly floured surface and pat it into a circle about 1 inch thick.
6. Use a round biscuit cutter to cut out scones and place them on the prepared baking sheet.
7. Bake for 15-18 minutes or until the scones are golden brown.
8. Allow the scones to cool slightly before serving.

Mr. Collins'
Cucumber
Sandwiches

Ingredients:
- 1 English cucumber, thinly sliced
- 8 ounces cream cheese, softened
- 1 tablespoon fresh dill, chopped
- Salt and pepper to taste
- 12 slices of white or whole wheat bread, crusts removed

Instructions:
1. In a bowl, combine the softened cream cheese and chopped dill. Season with salt and pepper to taste.
2. Spread a thin layer of the cream cheese mixture on each slice of bread.
3. Arrange the thinly sliced cucumber on half of the bread slices.
4. Top with the remaining slices to create sandwiches.
5. Cut each sandwich into desired shapes, such as triangles or rectangles.

Elizabeth's Lemon Lavender Tea Cake

Ingredients:

- 1 cup unsalted butter, softened
- 1 1/2 cups granulated sugar
- 4 large eggs
- 2 cups all-purpose flour
- 1 teaspoon baking powder
- 1/2 teaspoon baking soda
- 1/2 teaspoon salt
- 1/2 cup buttermilk
- Zest of 2 lemons
- 1 tablespoon dried lavender buds

Instructions:

1. Preheat your oven to 350°F (175°C) and grease a loaf pan.
2. In a large bowl, cream together the butter and sugar until light and fluffy.
3. Add the eggs one at a time, beating well after each addition.
4. In a separate bowl, whisk together the flour, baking powder, baking soda, and salt.
5. Gradually add the dry ingredients to the butter mixture, alternating with the buttermilk. Begin and end with the dry ingredients.
6. Stir in the lemon zest and dried lavender buds.
7. Pour the batter into the prepared loaf pan and smooth the top.
8. Bake for 50-60 minutes or until a toothpick inserted into the center comes out clean.
9. Allow the tea cake to cool in the pan for 15 minutes before transferring it to a wire rack to cool completely.

Meryton Mornings: Breakfast Delights with the Bennet Sisters

Jane's Honeyed Oatmeal with Berries

Ingredients:

- 1 cup rolled oats
- 2 cups milk (or water)
- 2 tablespoons honey
- Fresh berries (strawberries, blueberries, or raspberries)
- Chopped nuts for garnish

Instructions:
- Cook the oats according to package instructions, using milk for added creaminess.
- Drizzle honey over the cooked oatmeal.
- Top with fresh berries and garnish with chopped nuts.

Lydia's Peach and Prosciutto Croissant Sandwiches

Ingredients:

- Fresh croissants, sliced
- Sliced ripe peaches
- Prosciutto
- Goat cheese
- Arugula leaves

Instructions:

- Slice the croissants and spread goat cheese on each half.
- Layer prosciutto, sliced peaches, and arugula between the croissant halves.

Pemberley Garden Luncheon: Fresh Fare Fit for Mr. Darcy

Darcy's Deviled Eggs

Ingredients:
- 6 hard-boiled eggs, peeled and halved
- 3 tablespoons mayonnaise
- 1 teaspoon Dijon mustard
- 1 teaspoon white wine vinegar
- Salt and pepper to taste
- Paprika for garnish
- Fresh chives, finely chopped, for garnish

Instructions:
1. Remove the yolks from the halved eggs and place them in a bowl.
2. Mash the yolks and mix in mayonnaise, Dijon mustard, white wine vinegar, salt, and pepper until smooth.
3. Spoon or pipe the yolk mixture back into the egg whites.
4. Sprinkle with paprika and garnish with fresh chives.

Pemberley Salad with Raspberry Vinaigrette

Ingredients for Salad:

- Mixed salad greens (spinach, arugula, and watercress)
- Sliced strawberries
- Candied pecans
- Feta cheese, crumbled

Ingredients for Raspberry Vinaigrette:
- 1/2 cup fresh raspberries
- 1/4 cup olive oil
- 2 tablespoons balsamic vinegar
- 1 tablespoon honey
- Salt and pepper to taste

Instructions:
1. In a blender, combine raspberries, olive oil, balsamic vinegar, honey, salt, and pepper. Blend until smooth.
2. In a large bowl, toss the mixed salad greens with sliced strawberries, candied pecans, and crumbled feta cheese.
3. Drizzle the raspberry vinaigrette over the salad just before serving.

Fitzwilliam's Earl Grey Lavender Tea

Ingredients:

- 1 Earl Grey tea bag
- 1 teaspoon dried lavender buds
- Honey or sugar to taste
- Lemon slices for garnish (optional)

Instructions:

1. Steep the Earl Grey tea bag and dried lavender buds in hot water for 3-5 minutes.
2. Remove the tea bag and strain out the lavender buds.
3. Sweeten with honey or sugar to taste.
4. Garnish with lemon slices if desired.

Enjoy this Pemberley Garden Luncheon inspired by Mr. Darcy's refined tastes. These recipes bring a touch of elegance and freshness to your table, making every bite a nod to the sophistication of Austen's world. Happy cooking!

"I shall be miserable if I have not an excellent library."

- Pride and Prejudice

Pemberley Feast: Elegant Dinner with Mr. Darcy and Elizabeth

Darcy's Beef Wellington

- Ingredients:

  - Beef tenderloin
  - Salt and pepper to taste
  - Olive oil
  - Dijon mustard
  - Mushroom duxelles (finely chopped mushrooms, garlic, and herbs)
  - Puff pastry sheets
  - Egg wash (1 egg beaten with a little water)

- Instructions:

  - Season the beef with salt and pepper and sear on all sides in a hot skillet with olive oil.
  - Brush the beef with Dijon mustard.
  - Coat the beef with mushroom duxelles.
  - Roll out puff pastry and wrap it around the beef.
  - Brush with egg wash and bake at 400°F (200°C) until the pastry is golden brown.

Elizabeth's Garden Salad with Herb Vinaigrette

- Ingredients:
    - Mixed salad greens (arugula, spinach, and watercress)
    - Cherry tomatoes, halved
    - Cucumber, thinly sliced
    - Red onion, thinly sliced
    - Feta cheese, crumbled
- Herb Vinaigrette:
    - 1/4 cup extra virgin olive oil
    - 2 tablespoons balsamic vinegar
    - 1 teaspoon Dijon mustard
    - 1 tablespoon fresh herbs (parsley, basil, or thyme), chopped
    - Salt and pepper to taste
- Instructions:
    - In a large bowl, combine the salad greens, cherry tomatoes, cucumber, red onion, and feta cheese.
    - In a separate bowl, whisk together the olive oil, balsamic vinegar, Dijon mustard, fresh herbs, salt, and pepper.
    - Drizzle the vinaigrette over the salad just before serving.

"To be fond of dancing was a certain step towards falling in love."

- Pride and Prejudice

Rosings Park Roasts: Hearty Dinners with Lady Catherine de Bourgh

Lady Catherine's Rosemary Roast Lamb

- Ingredients:

    - Leg of lamb
    - Garlic cloves, minced
    - Fresh rosemary, chopped
    - Olive oil
    - Salt and pepper to taste

- Instructions:

    - Preheat the oven to 325°F (160°C).
    - Make small incisions in the lamb and insert minced garlic.
    - Rub the lamb with olive oil, chopped rosemary, salt, and pepper.
    - Roast until the internal temperature reaches your desired level of doneness.

Colonel Fitzwilliam's Balsamic Glazed Brussels Sprouts

- Ingredients:

    - Brussels sprouts, halved
    - Olive oil
    - Balsamic vinegar
    - Honey
    - Salt and pepper to taste

- Instructions:

    - Roast halved Brussels sprouts in olive oil until golden.
    - Drizzle with a mixture of balsamic vinegar and honey.
    - Season with salt and pepper to taste.

Hartfield High Tea: Emma's Social Delights

Mr. Woodhouse's Cinnamon Apple Muffins

Ingredients:

- 2 cups all-purpose flour
- 1 cup granulated sugar
- 1 tablespoon baking powder
- 1/2 teaspoon baking soda
- 1/2 teaspoon salt
- 1 teaspoon ground cinnamon
- 1 cup unsweetened applesauce
- 1/2 cup unsalted butter, melted and cooled
- 2 large eggs
- 1 teaspoon vanilla extract
- 1 cup diced apples (peeled and cored)
- Powdered sugar for dusting (optional)

Instructions:

1. Preheat your oven to 375°F (190°C) and line a muffin tin with paper liners.
2. In a large bowl, whisk together the flour, sugar, baking powder, baking soda, salt, and cinnamon.
3. In a separate bowl, mix together the applesauce, melted butter, eggs, and vanilla extract.
4. Combine the wet ingredients with the dry ingredients until just combined.
5. Fold in the diced apples.
6. Spoon the batter into the muffin cups, filling each about two-thirds full.
7. Bake for 18-20 minutes or until a toothpick inserted into the center comes out clean.
8. Allow the muffins to cool for a few minutes before transferring them to a wire rack. Dust with powdered sugar if desired.

Harriet's Apricot Tartlets

Ingredients:
- 1 sheet of puff pastry, thawed
- 1/2 cup apricot preserves
- Fresh apricots, sliced
- Slivered almonds for garnish
- Powdered sugar for dusting

Instructions:

1. Preheat your oven to 400°F (200°C).
2. Roll out the puff pastry and cut it into squares or circles, depending on your preference.
3. Place the pastry pieces on a baking sheet lined with parchment paper.
4. Spread a thin layer of apricot preserves on each pastry piece.
5. Arrange fresh apricot slices on top and sprinkle with slivered almonds.
6. Bake for 15-18 minutes or until the pastry is golden brown.
7. Allow the tartlets to cool slightly before dusting with powdered sugar.

Emma's Garden Party Infusion

Ingredients:

- 2 chamomile tea bags
- 1 teaspoon dried rose petals
- 1 cup hot water
- 1/4 cup vanilla-flavored almond milk
- 1 tablespoon honey
- Edible flowers for garnish

Instructions:

1. Steep the chamomile tea bags and dried rose petals in hot water for 4-5 minutes.
2. While steeping, heat the vanilla-flavored almond milk until warm.
3. Remove the tea bags and rose petals, then combine the chamomile infusion with the warm almond milk.
4. Stir in honey to sweeten, adjusting to your taste preference.
5. Pour the Garden Party Infusion into delicate teacups.
6. Garnish with edible flowers for a touch of whimsy.

Emma's Elegant Apple Pie

Ingredients

For the Pie Crust:
- 2 1/2 cups all-purpose flour
- 1 cup unsalted butter, chilled and cubed
- 1 teaspoon salt
- 1 tablespoon granulated sugar
- 1/4 to 1/2 cup ice water

For the Apple Filling:
- 6 large apples (a mix of sweet and tart varieties), peeled, cored, and thinly sliced
- 1/2 cup granulated sugar
- 1/2 cup light brown sugar, packed
- 1 teaspoon ground cinnamon
- 1/4 teaspoon ground nutmeg
- 2 tablespoons all-purpose flour
- 1 tablespoon lemon juice

For Assembly:
- 1 tablespoon unsalted butter, cut into small pieces (for dotting)
- 1 egg (for egg wash)
- 1 tablespoon turbinado sugar (for sprinkling)

Emma's Elegant Apple Pie

Instructions:

1. Prepare the Pie Crust:
- In a large bowl, combine the flour, salt, and sugar.
- Add the chilled butter cubes and use a pastry cutter or your fingers to work the butter into the flour until it resembles coarse crumbs.
- Gradually add ice water, a tablespoon at a time, and mix until the dough comes together.
- Divide the dough in half, shape each into a disc, wrap in plastic wrap, and refrigerate for at least 1 hour.

2. Preheat the Oven: Preheat your oven to 375°F (190°C).

3. Prepare the Apple Filling:
- In a large bowl, combine the sliced apples, granulated sugar, brown sugar, cinnamon, nutmeg, flour, and lemon juice. Toss until the apples are evenly coated.

4. Roll Out the Pie Crust:
- On a lightly floured surface, roll out one disc of the chilled pie dough to fit a 9-inch pie dish.
- Place the rolled-out crust into the pie dish, gently pressing it into the corners.

5. Add the Apple Filling:
- Pour the prepared apple filling into the pie crust, spreading it evenly.
- Dot the top of the filling with small pieces of unsalted butter.

6. Roll Out the Top Crust:
- Roll out the second disc of pie dough and place it over the apple filling.
- Trim and crimp the edges to seal the pie.

7. Make Slits and Brush with Egg Wash:
- Cut slits in the top crust to allow steam to escape.
- Beat the egg and brush it over the top crust for a golden finish.
- Sprinkle turbinado sugar over the egg wash.

8. Bake: Place the pie on a baking sheet to catch any drips and bake in the preheated oven for about 50-60 minutes or until the crust is golden brown, and the filling is bubbly.

9. Cool and Serve: Allow the pie to cool for at least 2 hours before slicing. Serve with a dollop of whipped cream or a scoop of vanilla ice cream.

"Good apple pies are a considerable part of our domestic happiness." - Emma

Mansfield Park Soiree: Elegant Evening Entrees

Sir Thomas Bertram's Roast Chicken

Ingredients:

- 1 whole roasting chicken (about 4-5 pounds)
- 2 tablespoons olive oil
- 1 teaspoon dried thyme
- 1 teaspoon dried rosemary
- 1 teaspoon garlic powder
- Salt and pepper to taste
- Lemon wedges for serving

Instructions:

1. Preheat your oven to 375°F (190°C).
2. Rinse the chicken and pat it dry with paper towels.
3. In a small bowl, mix together olive oil, thyme, rosemary, garlic powder, salt, and pepper.
4. Rub the spice mixture all over the chicken, ensuring it's evenly coated.
5. Place the chicken on a roasting pan and roast in the preheated oven for about 1.5 to 2 hours or until the internal temperature reaches 165°F (74°C).
6. Allow the chicken to rest for 10 minutes before carving.
7. Serve with lemon wedges on the side.

Fanny Price's Mushroom Risotto

Ingredients:
- 1 cup Arborio rice
- 1/2 cup dry white wine
- 4 cups chicken or vegetable broth, kept warm
- 1 cup mushrooms, sliced (shiitake or cremini)
- 1 small onion, finely chopped
- 2 cloves garlic, minced
- 1/2 cup Parmesan cheese, grated
- 2 tablespoons unsalted butter
- Salt and pepper to taste
- Fresh parsley for garnish

Instructions:
1. In a large pan, sauté the onions and garlic in butter until softened.
2. Add the Arborio rice and cook, stirring, for 2-3 minutes until the rice is lightly toasted.
3. Pour in the white wine and cook until it's mostly absorbed.
4. Begin adding the warm broth one ladle at a time, stirring frequently and allowing the liquid to be absorbed before adding more.
5. When the rice is almost cooked, add the sliced mushrooms.
6. Continue adding broth until the rice is creamy and cooked to al dente.
7. Stir in Parmesan cheese, salt, and pepper.
8. Garnish with fresh parsley before serving.

Edmund's Blackcurrant Cordial

Ingredients:

- 1 cup blackcurrants (fresh or frozen)
- 1 cup water
- 1/2 cup granulated sugar
- 1 tablespoon lemon juice
- Sparkling water or still water for serving
- Ice cubes
- Fresh blackcurrants and mint leaves for garnish

Instructions:

1. In a saucepan, combine blackcurrants, water, sugar, and lemon juice.
2. Bring to a simmer over medium heat, stirring until the sugar dissolves.
3. Simmer for about 10 minutes, then strain the mixture to remove seeds and pulp.
4. Allow the blackcurrant syrup to cool.
5. To serve, mix 2-3 tablespoons of blackcurrant syrup with sparkling or still water.
6. Add ice cubes and garnish with fresh blackcurrants and mint leaves.

"To sit in the shade on a fine day and look upon verdure is the most perfect refreshment."

- Mansfield Park

Northanger Abbey Sweet Indulgences: Desserts with Catherine Morland

Bath Buns with Clotted Cream

Ingredients:
- 4 cups all-purpose flour
- 1/2 cup granulated sugar
- 1 tablespoon active dry yeast
- 1 teaspoon salt
- 1 cup warm milk
- 1/2 cup unsalted butter, softened
- 2 large eggs
- 1/2 cup currants or raisins
- Clotted cream for serving

Instructions:
1. In a bowl, combine warm milk, sugar, and yeast. Let it sit until frothy.
2. In a large mixing bowl, combine flour and salt. Add the yeast mixture, softened butter, and eggs. Mix until a dough forms.
3. Knead the dough on a floured surface for about 10 minutes or until smooth and elastic.
4. Place the dough in a greased bowl, cover with a damp cloth, and let it rise in a warm place until doubled in size.
5. Punch down the dough and knead in currants or raisins.
6. Divide the dough into equal portions and shape into buns. Place them on a baking sheet.
7. Let the buns rise for another 30 minutes.
8. Bake in a preheated oven at 375°F (190°C) for 15-20 minutes or until golden brown.
9. Serve with clotted cream.

Henry Tilney's Lavender-infused Custard

Ingredients:

- 2 cups whole milk
- 1/2 cup granulated sugar
- 1 vanilla bean, split and seeds scraped (or 1 teaspoon vanilla extract)
- 2 tablespoons dried lavender buds
- 6 large egg yolks

Instructions:

1. In a saucepan, heat the milk, sugar, vanilla bean (or extract), and lavender over medium heat until it just starts to simmer. Remove from heat.
2. In a bowl, whisk the egg yolks. Gradually pour the hot milk mixture into the egg yolks, whisking constantly.
3. Return the mixture to the saucepan and cook over low heat, stirring continuously until the custard thickens (do not let it boil).
4. Strain the custard through a fine-mesh sieve to remove the lavender buds and any curdled bits.
5. Chill the custard in the refrigerator for at least 4 hours or until cold.
6. Serve in individual cups, garnished with a sprig of fresh lavender if available.

Mrs. Allen's Lemon Posset

Ingredients:

- 2 cups heavy cream
- 3/4 cup granulated sugar
- 1/3 cup fresh lemon juice
- Lemon zest for garnish

Instructions:

1. In a saucepan, heat the heavy cream and sugar over medium heat, stirring until the sugar dissolves.
2. Bring the mixture to a gentle simmer and continue to cook for 5 minutes.
3. Remove from heat and stir in the fresh lemon juice.
4. Let the mixture cool for a few minutes, then strain to remove any curdled bits.
5. Pour the posset into serving glasses and refrigerate for at least 4 hours or until set.
6. Garnish with lemon zest before serving.

Persuasion Picnic: Seaside Delicacies with Anne Elliot

Captain Wentworth's Seafood Pâté

Ingredients:

- 8 ounces cream cheese, softened
- 1/2 cup mayonnaise
- 1 tablespoon Dijon mustard
- 1 tablespoon lemon juice
- 1/2 teaspoon Worcestershire sauce
- 1/2 teaspoon hot sauce (adjust to taste)
- 1 cup mixed seafood (shrimp, crab, or lobster), cooked and finely chopped
- Salt and pepper to taste
- Fresh parsley for garnish
- Crackers or baguette slices for serving

Instructions:

1. In a bowl, combine softened cream cheese, mayonnaise, Dijon mustard, lemon juice, Worcestershire sauce, and hot sauce. Mix until smooth.
2. Fold in the finely chopped seafood.
3. Season with salt and pepper to taste.
4. Transfer the seafood pâté to a serving dish, garnish with fresh parsley, and refrigerate for at least 1 hour before serving.
5. Serve with crackers or slices of baguette.

Lyme Regis Lobster Salad

Ingredients:

- 1 pound cooked lobster meat, diced
- 1/2 cup mayonnaise
- 1 celery stalk, finely chopped
- 1 tablespoon fresh chives, chopped
- 1 tablespoon fresh tarragon, chopped
- Zest and juice of 1 lemon
- Salt and pepper to taste
- Butter lettuce leaves for serving

Instructions:

1. In a bowl, combine diced lobster meat, mayonnaise, chopped celery, chives, tarragon, lemon zest, and lemon juice. Mix well.
2. Season with salt and pepper to taste.
3. Refrigerate the lobster salad for at least 30 minutes before serving.
4. Serve the lobster salad in butter lettuce leaves for a refreshing and elegant presentation.

Admiral Croft's Ginger Beer

Ingredients:

- 1 cup fresh ginger, peeled and grated
- 1 cup brown sugar
- 1 cup water
- Juice of 2 lemons
- 1/4 teaspoon active dry yeast
- 4 cups cold water
- Ice cubes
- Lemon slices and fresh mint for garnish

Instructions:

1. In a saucepan, combine grated ginger, brown sugar, and 1 cup of water. Bring to a simmer and let it cook for 10 minutes.
2. Remove from heat and let the ginger mixture cool to room temperature.
3. Strain the ginger syrup into a large pitcher.
4. In a small bowl, dissolve the yeast in 1/4 cup of warm water and let it sit for 5 minutes.
5. Add the yeast mixture, lemon juice, and 4 cups of cold water to the ginger syrup. Mix well.
6. Refrigerate the ginger beer for at least 2 hours.
7. Serve over ice, garnished with lemon slices and fresh mint.

Bath Assembly Bakes: Delicacies from Northanger Abbey

Catherine Morland's Lavender Shortbread

Ingredients:

- 1 cup unsalted butter, softened
- 1/2 cup powdered sugar
- 2 cups all-purpose flour
- 1 tablespoon dried lavender buds (culinary grade)
- 1/4 teaspoon salt
- Lavender sugar for sprinkling (optional)

Instructions:

1. Preheat your oven to 325°F (163°C) and line a baking sheet with parchment paper.
2. In a bowl, cream together softened butter and powdered sugar until light and fluffy.
3. In a separate bowl, whisk together the flour, dried lavender buds, and salt.
4. Gradually add the dry ingredients to the butter mixture, mixing until just combined.
5. Roll the dough into a log shape and wrap it in plastic wrap. Chill in the refrigerator for at least 30 minutes.
6. Slice the chilled dough into rounds and place them on the prepared baking sheet.
7. Optional: Sprinkle each shortbread round with lavender sugar.
8. Bake for 12-15 minutes or until the edges are lightly golden.
9. Allow the lavender shortbread to cool on the baking sheet before transferring to a wire rack.

Tilney's Tea Cakes

Ingredients:

For the Tea Cakes:

- 2 cups all-purpose flour
- 1 1/2 teaspoons baking powder
- 1/4 teaspoon salt
- 1/2 cup unsalted butter, softened
- 1 cup granulated sugar
- 2 large eggs
- 1 teaspoon vanilla extract
- 1/2 cup whole milk

For the Glaze:

- 2 cups powdered sugar
- 2-3 tablespoons milk
- 1 teaspoon lemon zest
- Edible flowers for garnish

Instructions:

1. Preheat your oven to 350°F (175°C) and grease a bundt cake pan.
2. In a bowl, whisk together the flour, baking powder, and salt.
3. In a separate large bowl, cream together the softened butter and sugar until light and fluffy.
4. Add the eggs one at a time, beating well after each addition. Stir in the vanilla extract.
5. Gradually add the dry ingredients to the wet ingredients, alternating with the milk, beginning and ending with the dry ingredients. Mix until just combined.
6. Pour the batter into the greased bundt cake pan and bake for 40-45 minutes or until a toothpick inserted into the center comes out clean.
7. Let the tea cake cool in the pan for 10 minutes before transferring it to a wire rack to cool completely.
8. For the glaze, whisk together powdered sugar, milk, and lemon zest until smooth. Drizzle the glaze over the cooled tea cake.
9. Garnish with edible flowers for a decorative touch.

Eleanor's Elderflower & Lemon Madeleines

Ingredients:

- 2/3 cup all-purpose flour
- 1/2 teaspoon baking powder
- 1/4 teaspoon salt
- 1/2 cup unsalted butter, melted and cooled
- 2 large eggs
- 1/2 cup granulated sugar
- Zest of 1 lemon
- 1 tablespoon elderflower cordial
- Powdered sugar for dusting

Instructions:

1. Preheat your oven to 375°F (190°C) and grease madeleine molds.
2. In a bowl, whisk together flour, baking powder, and salt.
3. In another bowl, beat eggs and sugar until light and fluffy.
4. Gently fold in the melted butter, lemon zest, and elderflower cordial.
5. Gradually add the dry ingredients to the wet ingredients, mixing until just combined.
6. Spoon the batter into the madeleine molds.
7. Bake for 10-12 minutes or until the madeleines are golden brown and have a slight hump.
8. Allow them to cool before dusting with powdered sugar.

Dashwood Desserts: Sweet Temptations from Sense and Sensibility

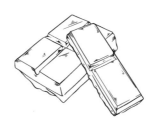

Marianne's Honeyed Almonds

Ingredients:

- 1 cup whole almonds
- 2 tablespoons honey
- 1 tablespoon unsalted butter
- 1/2 teaspoon sea salt

Instructions:

1. Preheat your oven to 350°F (175°C) and line a baking sheet with parchment paper.
2. In a saucepan over medium heat, melt the butter and honey together.
3. Add the almonds to the saucepan, stirring to coat them in the honey-butter mixture.
4. Spread the almonds on the prepared baking sheet in a single layer.
5. Sprinkle with sea salt.
6. Bake for 10-12 minutes, stirring halfway through, until the almonds are golden brown.
7. Allow the honeyed almonds to cool completely before serving.

Colonel Brandon's Dark Chocolate Mousse

Ingredients:

- 8 ounces dark chocolate, chopped
- 1/4 cup strong brewed coffee, cooled
- 3 large eggs, separated
- 1/4 cup granulated sugar
- 1 cup heavy cream
- Dark chocolate shavings for garnish

Instructions:

1. Melt the dark chocolate in a heatproof bowl set over a pot of simmering water (double boiler). Once melted, remove from heat.
2. Stir the brewed coffee into the melted chocolate and let it cool to room temperature.
3. In a separate bowl, beat the egg yolks with half of the sugar until pale and creamy. Add the chocolate-coffee mixture and mix until smooth.
4. In another bowl, whip the egg whites until soft peaks form. Gradually add the remaining sugar and continue whipping until stiff peaks form.
5. Gently fold the whipped egg whites into the chocolate mixture until well combined.
6. Whip the heavy cream until stiff peaks form. Fold it into the chocolate mixture.
7. Spoon the mousse into serving glasses or bowls and refrigerate for at least 2 hours.
8. Garnish with dark chocolate shavings before serving.

Elinor's Orange Blossom Cake

Ingredients:

For the Cake:

- 2 cups all-purpose flour
- 1 1/2 teaspoons baking powder
- 1/2 teaspoon baking soda
- 1/4 teaspoon salt
- 1/2 cup unsalted butter, softened
- 1 cup granulated sugar
- 2 large eggs
- 1 teaspoon vanilla extract
- Zest of 1 orange
- 1 cup buttermilk

For the Orange Blossom Glaze:

- 1 cup powdered sugar
- 2 tablespoons fresh orange juice
- 1 teaspoon orange blossom water

Instructions:

1. Preheat your oven to 350°F (175°C) and grease and flour a cake pan.
2. In a bowl, whisk together the flour, baking powder, baking soda, and salt.
3. In another large bowl, cream together the softened butter and sugar until light and fluffy.
4. Add the eggs one at a time, beating well after each addition. Stir in the vanilla extract and orange zest.
5. Gradually add the dry ingredients to the wet ingredients, alternating with the buttermilk, beginning and ending with the dry ingredients. Mix until just combined.
6. Pour the batter into the prepared cake pan and bake for 25-30 minutes or until a toothpick inserted into the center comes out clean.
7. While the cake is baking, prepare the orange blossom glaze by whisking together powdered sugar, fresh orange juice, and orange blossom water.
8. Allow the cake to cool in the pan for 10 minutes, then transfer it to a wire rack to cool completely. Drizzle the orange blossom glaze over the cooled cake.

"I am excessively fond of a cottage; there is always so much comfort, so much elegance about them. And I protest, if I had any money to spare, I should buy a little land and build one myself, within a short distance of London, where I might drive myself down at any time, and collect a few friends about me, and be happy. I advise everybody who is going to build, to build a cottage."

- Sense and Sensibility

Emma's Garden Feast: Seasonal Delights from Highbury

Mr. Woodhouse's Cucumber Mint Sandwiches

Ingredients:

- 1 large cucumber, thinly sliced
- 8 ounces cream cheese, softened
- 2 tablespoons fresh mint, finely chopped
- Salt and pepper to taste
- 8 slices of white or whole wheat bread

Instructions:

1. In a bowl, mix the softened cream cheese with chopped mint until well combined.
2. Season the cream cheese mixture with salt and pepper to taste.
3. Spread a generous layer of the minted cream cheese on each slice of bread.
4. Arrange thinly sliced cucumber on half of the bread slices.
5. Top with the remaining bread slices to form sandwiches.
6. Trim the crusts if desired and cut each sandwich into halves or quarters.
7. Serve chilled and enjoy the refreshing combination of cucumber and mint.

Mr. Knightley's Asparagus and Lemon Risotto

Ingredients:
- 1 cup Arborio rice
- 2 cups asparagus, trimmed and cut into bite-sized pieces
- 1 onion, finely chopped
- 2 cloves garlic, minced
- 4 cups vegetable or chicken broth, kept warm
- 1 cup dry white wine
- Zest of 1 lemon
- Juice of 1 lemon
- 1/2 cup Parmesan cheese, grated
- 2 tablespoons butter
- Salt and pepper to taste
- Fresh parsley for garnish

Instructions:
1. In a large pan, sauté the chopped onion and minced garlic in olive oil until softened.
2. Add Arborio rice and cook, stirring, until the rice is lightly toasted.
3. Pour in the white wine and stir until absorbed by the rice.
4. Begin adding warm broth, one ladle at a time, stirring frequently. Allow the liquid to be absorbed before adding more.
5. When the rice is almost tender, add the asparagus and continue cooking until the asparagus is bright green and crisp-tender.
6. Stir in lemon zest, lemon juice, Parmesan cheese, and butter. Season with salt and pepper to taste.
7. Garnish with fresh parsley before serving. The risotto should be creamy with a slight bite to the rice.

Hartfield Herb-infused Lemonade

Ingredients:
- 1 cup fresh lemon juice (about 6 lemons)
- 1 cup granulated sugar (adjust to taste)
- 6 cups cold water
- Handful of fresh herbs (e.g., mint, basil, or lemon balm)
- Lemon slices and fresh herb sprigs for garnish
- Ice cubes

Instructions:
1. In a small saucepan, combine sugar with 1 cup of water. Heat over medium heat, stirring until sugar dissolves to create a simple syrup. Let it cool.
2. In a large pitcher, combine fresh lemon juice and the simple syrup.
3. Add cold water to the lemon mixture, adjusting to your preferred level of sweetness.
4. Gently bruise the fresh herbs by crushing them with a muddler or the back of a spoon. Add them to the lemonade.
5. Refrigerate the lemonade for at least 1-2 hours to allow the flavors to meld.
6. Before serving, strain out the herbs, leaving a clear lemonade.
7. Serve over ice, garnished with lemon slices and fresh herb sprigs.

"You must allow me to tell you how ardently I admire and love you."

-Pride and Prejudice

Regency Revelry Cocktails: Libations for Social Soirées

Ballroom Punch with Rose Petal Ice Cubes

Ingredients:

For the Punch:

- 1 cup black tea, cooled
- 1 cup gin
- 1/2 cup elderflower liqueur
- 1/2 cup raspberry syrup
- 1/4 cup fresh lemon juice
- 1 bottle sparkling water or Champagne

For the Rose Petal Ice Cubes:

- Edible rose petals
- Water

Instructions:

For the Rose Petal Ice Cubes:
1. Place one edible rose petal in each compartment of an ice cube tray.
2. Fill the tray with water and freeze until solid.

For the Punch:
1. In a punch bowl, combine cooled black tea, gin, elderflower liqueur, raspberry syrup, and fresh lemon juice.
2. Just before serving, add rose petal ice cubes.
3. Top with sparkling water or Champagne.
4. Stir gently and serve.

Pimm's Cup for a Summer Garden Party

Ingredients:

- 2 cups Pimm's No. 1
- 4 cups ginger ale
- Sliced cucumber
- Sliced strawberries
- Orange slices
- Fresh mint leaves
- Ice cubes

Instructions:

1. Fill a pitcher with ice cubes.
2. Add Pimm's No. 1 and ginger ale to the pitcher.
3. Stir gently to combine.
4. Add sliced cucumber, strawberries, orange slices, and fresh mint leaves to the pitcher.
5. Stir again and let it chill in the refrigerator for at least 30 minutes.
6. Serve over ice in individual glasses.

Mr. Bingley's Blackberry Bramble

Ingredients:

- 2 oz gin
- 1 oz blackberry liqueur
- 3/4 oz fresh lemon juice
- 1/2 oz simple syrup
- Fresh blackberries for garnish

Instructions:

1. In a shaker, combine gin, blackberry liqueur, fresh lemon juice, and simple syrup.
2. Fill the shaker with ice and shake well.
3. Strain the mixture into a glass filled with crushed ice.
4. Garnish with fresh blackberries.
5. Optionally, add a lemon twist for extra zest.

"One cannot have too large a party. A large party secures its own amusement."

- Emma

Beyond the Ballroom: Late-Night Nibbles for Austen-Inspired Gatherings

Midnight Macarons with Lavender Ganache

Ingredients: For the Macarons:

- 1 cup almond flour
- 1 3/4 cups powdered sugar
- 3 large egg whites, room temperature
- 1/4 cup granulated sugar
- Purple food coloring (optional)

For the Lavender Ganache:

- 1/2 cup heavy cream
- 1 tablespoon dried lavender buds
- 6 ounces white chocolate, finely chopped
- Purple food coloring (optional)

Instructions: For the Macarons:

1. Line baking sheets with parchment paper.
2. In a food processor, combine almond flour and powdered sugar. Pulse until fine.
3. In a bowl, whip egg whites until foamy. Gradually add granulated sugar, continuing to whip until stiff peaks form.
4. Gently fold the almond mixture into the whipped egg whites. Add food coloring if desired.
5. Transfer the batter to a piping bag and pipe small circles onto the prepared baking sheets.
6. Let the macarons sit at room temperature for 30 minutes to form a skin.
7. Preheat the oven to 300°F (150°C) and bake for 15-18 minutes.
8. Let the macarons cool completely before filling.

For the Lavender Ganache:

1. In a small saucepan, heat the heavy cream and dried lavender buds over medium heat until it begins to simmer.
2. Remove from heat and let it steep for 15 minutes. Strain out the lavender buds.
3. Reheat the cream and pour it over the finely chopped white chocolate. Let it sit for a minute and then stir until smooth.
4. Add purple food coloring if desired.
5. Let the ganache cool and thicken before using it to sandwich the macarons.

Sir Walter Elliot's Truffle Oil Popcorn

Ingredients:

- 1/2 cup popcorn kernels
- 2 tablespoons truffle oil
- 2 tablespoons melted butter
- 1/4 cup grated Parmesan cheese
- Salt to taste
- Fresh parsley, finely chopped (for garnish)

Instructions:

1. Pop the popcorn kernels using your preferred method.
2. In a large bowl, combine truffle oil and melted butter.
3. Add the popped popcorn to the bowl and toss to coat evenly with the truffle oil and butter mixture.
4. Sprinkle grated Parmesan cheese and salt over the popcorn, tossing again to distribute.
5. Garnish with fresh parsley and serve immediately.

Wickham's Whiskey-infused Nuts

Ingredients:

- 2 cups mixed nuts (almonds, walnuts, pecans)
- 2 tablespoons whiskey
- 2 tablespoons brown sugar
- 1 teaspoon smoked paprika
- 1/2 teaspoon cayenne pepper
- 1 teaspoon sea salt

Instructions:

1. Preheat the oven to 325°F (160°C) and line a baking sheet with parchment paper.
2. In a bowl, mix the whiskey, brown sugar, smoked paprika, cayenne pepper, and sea salt.
3. Add the mixed nuts to the bowl and toss to coat evenly with the whiskey mixture.
4. Spread the nuts in a single layer on the prepared baking sheet.
5. Bake for 15-20 minutes, stirring halfway through, until the nuts are golden and fragrant.
6. Allow the nuts to cool completely before serving.

CLOSING REFLECTION

In the grand tapestry of Austen's world, where social graces and delightful repasts intertwine, we bid you farewell from our Regency-inspired kitchen. As you close this book, may the aroma of these recipes linger in your senses, transporting you to a time of elegance, wit, and the simple joys found around a well-laid table. In the company of characters like Elizabeth Bennet, Emma Woodhouse, and Anne Elliot, we've embarked on a culinary journey, savoring the flavors of a bygone era. Let these recipes be a constant companion, inviting you to recreate the charm of a Regency repast in your own home.

As Jane Austen once observed, 'Good company, good wine, good welcome can make good people.' May this collection of recipes and tales add a touch of goodness to your own gatherings. In the words of the great novelist herself, 'Ah! There is nothing like staying at home for real comfort.' So, find comfort in your kitchen, share laughter around your table, and relish the timeless joy of good food and good company.

Thank you for joining us on this culinary expedition through Austen's kitchen. Until we meet again, may your days be filled with the warmth of shared meals and the enduring magic of Jane Austen's world.

Dear Reader,

In the spirit of personalizing your culinary journey through Austen's kitchen, we invite you to make these pages your own. Use this space to pen down your musings, culinary experiments, and tales from your own kitchen adventures. Whether you've discovered a delightful twist to one of our recipes, wish to share your Regency-themed gatherings, or simply want to capture the essence of a memorable meal, these note pages are yours to fill.

Consider them your private canvas to document the flavors and moments inspired by the pages preceding them. Perhaps a quote from Austen stirred your imagination, or maybe a recipe sparked a delightful culinary revelation. Whatever it may be, let these notes be a testament to your unique journey through the world of Austen and the delicious creations it has inspired.

Happy cooking, scribing, and indulging!

Yours in Austen's culinary reverie,

Autumn Rosewood

MY NOTES

MY NOTES

MY NOTES

MY NOTES

MY NOTES

MY NOTES

MY NOTES

MY NOTES

MY NOTES

MY NOTES

MY NOTES

MY NOTES

MY NOTES

MY NOTES

MY NOTES

MY NOTES

MY NOTES

MY NOTES

MY NOTES

KITCHEN
Conversions

1 GALLON
4 QUARTZ
8 PINTS
16 CUPS
128 OZ

1 QUARTZ
2 PINTS
4 CUPS
32 OZ

1 PINT
2 CUPS
16 OZ

1 CUP
16 TBS
48 TSP
8 OZ

1/2 CUP
8 TBS
24 TSP
4 OZ

1/4 CUP
4 TBS
12 TSP
2 OZ

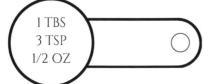

1 TBS
3 TSP
1/2 OZ

1 TBS
8 PINCHES

recipe card

○ ○ ○ ○ ○
DIFFICULTY

NAME OF DISH

CATEGORY

PREP TIME

COOK TIME

INGREDIENTS

- ....
- ....
- ....
- ....
- ....
- ....
- ....
- ....
- ....
- ....
- ....

directions

notes

recipe card

○ ○ ○ ○ ○
DIFFICULTY

NAME OF DISH

CATEGORY   PREP TIME   COOK TIME

INGREDIENTS

-
-
-
-
-
-
-
-
-
-
-

directions

notes

recipe card

○ ○ ○ ○ ○
DIFFICULTY

NAME OF DISH

CATEGORY

PREP TIME

COOK TIME

INGREDIENTS

-
-
-
-
-
-
-
-
-
-
-

directions

notes

recipe card

○ ○ ○ ○ ○
DIFFICULTY

NAME OF DISH

CATEGORY

PREP TIME

COOK TIME

INGREDIENTS

-
-
-
-
-
-
-
-
-
-

directions

notes

recipe card

○ ○ ○ ○ ○
DIFFICULTY

NAME OF DISH

CATEGORY   PREP TIME   COOK TIME

INGREDIENTS

directions

-
-
-
-
-
-
-
-
-
-
-

notes

recipe card

○ ○ ○ ○ ○
DIFFICULTY

NAME OF DISH

CATEGORY   **PREP TIME**   **COOK TIME**

INGREDIENTS

-
-
-
-
-
-
-
-
-
-
-

directions

notes

recipe card

○ ○ ○ ○ ○
DIFFICULTY

NAME OF DISH

CATEGORY

PREP TIME

COOK TIME

INGREDIENTS

- ....
- ....
- ....
- ....
- ....
- ....
- ....
- ....
- ....
- ....
- ....

directions

notes

recipe card

○ ○ ○ ○ ○
DIFFICULTY

NAME OF DISH

CATEGORY

PREP TIME

COOK TIME

INGREDIENTS

-
-
-
-
-
-
-
-
-
-
-

directions

notes

recipe card

NAME OF DISH

CATEGORY   PREP TIME   COOK TIME

INGREDIENTS

directions

-
-
-
-
-
-
-
-
-
-
-

notes

recipe card

○ ○ ○ ○ ○
DIFFICULTY

NAME OF DISH

CATEGORY

PREP TIME

COOK TIME

INGREDIENTS

- ....
- ....
- ....
- ....
- ....
- ....
- ....
- ....
- ....
- ....

directions

notes

Made in United States
Troutdale, OR
09/23/2024

23079155R00063